QUICK AND EASY
MICROWAVE
COOKBOOK

• BY •

CARLA HUTSON

Table of Contents

Steamed Fish With Herbs And Lemon

Fish is a tasty, nutritious, and versatile food that can be cooked in many different ways. One of the best ways to prepare it is by steaming it with herbs and lemon for added flavor. This simple and fast cooking method makes it an ideal choice for busy weeknights or when you want a quick and delicious meal.

TOTAL TIME PREP: 10-15 minutes.

Ingredients:

- 2 fish fillets, such as tilapia or sole
- 1/4 cup chopped fresh herbs, such as parsley, thyme, and oregano
- 1 lemon, sliced
- Salt and pepper to taste
- 2 tablespoons unsalted butter

Instructions:

1. Place the fish fillets in a microwave-safe dish.
2. Season the fish with salt and pepper to taste.
3. Top the fish fillets with the chopped fresh herbs.
4. Place the lemon slices on top of the herbs.
5. Add the butter to the dish, dividing it between the two fillets.
6. Cover the dish with a microwave-safe lid or plate and microwave on high for 3-4 minutes until the fish is cooked and flakes easily with a fork.
7. Let the fish cool for a few minutes before serving.
8. Serve with cooked rice.

Teriyaki Salmon With Sesame And Green Onions

Teriyaki Salmon with Sesame and Green Onions is a classic Japanese dish that is both nutritious and delicious. This meal is easy to make and can be served as an appetizer or main dish. Almost everyone loves teriyaki sauce's sweet, savory flavor combined with salmon, sesame seeds, and green onions. The unique combination of flavors makes this meal a favorite of home cooks all around the world.

TOTAL TIME PREP: 10-15 minutes.

Ingredients:

- 2 salmon fillets
- 1/4 cup teriyaki sauce
- 2 tablespoons sesame seeds
- 2 green onions, thinly sliced
- Salt and pepper to taste

Instructions:

1. Place the salmon fillets in a microwave-safe dish.
2. Season the salmon with salt and pepper to taste.
3. Pour the teriyaki sauce over the salmon fillets.
4. Sprinkle the sesame seeds and sliced green onions on top of the salmon.
5. Cover the dish with a microwave-safe lid or plate and microwave on high for 3-4 minutes until the salmon is cooked and flakes easily with a fork.
6. Let the salmon cool for a few minutes before serving.

Stir-Fried Squid with Salted Egg

Stir-fried squid with salted egg is a popular seafood dish in many Asian countries. It is a simple yet flavorful dish that brings together different ingredients to create a delicious meal. The combination of fresh squid and salted egg gives the dish its unique flavor profile and texture. Preparing this dish is relatively easy as it does not require complicated techniques.

TOTAL TIME PREP: 10-15 minutes.

Ingredients:

- 1 lb squid, cleaned and sliced
- 2 tablespoons vegetable oil
- 2 salted eggs, mashed
- 1 tablespoon chopped garlic
- 1 tablespoon chopped fresh chili pepper
- 1/2 teaspoon salt
- 1/4 teaspoon black pepper
- 2 tablespoons chopped fresh cilantro

Instructions:

1. In a microwave-safe dish, combine the squid, vegetable oil, mashed salted eggs, chopped garlic, chopped fresh chili pepper, salt, and black pepper.
2. Stir to combine.
3. Cover the dish with a microwave-safe lid or plate and microwave on high for 3-4 minutes, or until the squid is cooked through.
4. Remove the dish from the microwave and stir in the chopped fresh cilantro.
5. Serve the stir-fried squid immediately.

Pork Brown Rice Porridge

Pork brown rice porridge is a comforting and delicious dish perfect for any time of day. With its combination of tender pork, nutty brown rice and fragrant spices, it's sure to be a hit with the whole family. It's easy to make, too - this simple recipe requires just a few ingredients and minimal preparation. Its slow-cooked nature makes it ideal for busy weekday meals or relaxed weekend brunches.

TOTAL TIME PREP: 15-20 minutes.

Ingredients:

- 1 cup cooked brown rice
- 1/2 lb ground pork
- 2 cups water or chicken broth
- 1/2 onion, chopped
- 1 tablespoon chopped garlic
- 1 tablespoon chopped ginger
- 1 tablespoon soy sauce
- 1/2 teaspoon salt
- 1/4 teaspoon black pepper
- Sliced scallions and chopped fresh cilantro for garnish

Instructions:

1. In a microwave-safe dish, combine the cooked brown rice, ground pork, water or chicken broth, chopped onion, chopped garlic, chopped ginger, soy sauce, salt, and black pepper.
2. Stir to combine.
3. Cover the dish with a microwave-safe lid or plate and microwave on high for 10-12 minutes, stirring occasionally, or until the porridge is thick and creamy and the pork is cooked through.
4. Remove the dish from the microwave and let it sit for a few minutes before serving.
5. Garnish with sliced scallions and chopped fresh cilantro before serving.

Steamed Egg Noodles

Eggs and noodles are simple yet delicious dishes that can be cooked in various ways. From stir-frying to boiling, this combination of ingredients can be tailored to every taste. This recipe will discuss making the best-steamed egg and noodles by guiding you through the preparation steps. With some essential ingredients and a few simple techniques, you can easily create a flavorful meal in no time.

TOTAL TIME PREP: 30 minutes.

Ingredients:

For noodles:

- 2 bundles of dried egg noodles (about 6-8 oz)
- 1/2 cup chicken broth
- 2 tablespoons soy sauce
- 1 tablespoon oyster sauce
- 1 tablespoon vegetable oil
- 1 teaspoon sugar
- 1/4 teaspoon black pepper

For Steamed Egg:

- 1 large egg
- 1/2 cup chicken broth
- 1 tablespoon soy sauce
- 1/4 teaspoon salt
- 1/4 teaspoon black pepper
- Sliced green onions and sesame seeds for garnish

Instructions:

For Steamed Egg:

1. In a microwave-safe bowl, whisk together the eggs, soy sauce, salt, and black pepper until well combined.

2. Cover the bowl with a microwave-safe plate or lid and microwave on high for 1 minute and 30 seconds.
3. Check the egg to see if it has set. If it hasn't, microwave in 30-second increments until set. Once the egg is set, let it cool.

For noodles:

1. Place the dried noodles in a microwave-safe bowl and add enough water to cover the noodles. Microwave on high for 3-4 minutes, or until the noodles are cooked.
2. Drain the noodles and set aside.
3. In a separate microwave-safe bowl, whisk together the chicken broth, soy sauce, oyster sauce, vegetable oil, sugar, and black pepper.
4. Add the cooked noodles to the sauce mixture and toss to coat evenly.
5. Cover the bowl with a microwave-safe plate or lid and microwave on high for 1 minute and 30 seconds.
6. Remove the bowl from the microwave and stir the noodles.
7. Cover the bowl again and microwave for an additional 1 minute and 30 seconds.
8. Remove the bowl from the microwave. Place the Steamed Egg on the noodles and garnish with sliced green onions and sesame seeds.

Thai Steamed Tuna Curry (Homok)

Thai Steamed Tuna Curry is a delicious, quick and easy dish that can be enjoyed for lunch or dinner. This exotic curry has a combination of both sweet and savory flavors from the various spices used. The star of this dish is tuna, which is steamed in a flavorful coconut milk sauce. The sauce is made from herbs and spices, including lemongrass, galangal, and kaffir lime leaves.

TOTAL TIME PREP: 20 minutes.

Ingredients:

- 1 can (5 oz) of tuna, drained
- 1/4 cup coconut cream
- 1 egg
- 1 tablespoon red curry paste
- 1 tablespoon fish sauce
- 1 tablespoon sugar
- 1/4 cup sliced red bell pepper
- 1/4 cup basil
- 1/4 cup sliced cabbage or white cabbage
- Sliced kaffir lime leaves for garnish

Instructions:

1. In a microwave-safe bowl, whisk together the coconut cream, egg, red curry paste, fish sauce, and sugar until well combined.
2. Add the drained tuna, basil, cabbage and red bell pepper to the bowl and mix until everything is evenly distributed.
3. Cover the bowl with a microwave-safe plate or lid and microwave on high for 3-4 minutes, or until the mixture is cooked through and no longer jiggles when you shake the bowl.
4. Remove the bowl from the microwave and let it cool for a few minutes before garnishing it with sliced kaffir lime leaves.
5. Serve with cooked rice.

Steamed Snow Fish With Soy Sauce

Are you looking for a delicious and healthy Asian-style fish dish? Steamed snow fish with soy sauce is an easy, low-carb meal with plenty of flavors. Whether you're an experienced chef or a kitchen beginner, this dish will impress and delight your taste buds. The snow fish is perfectly steamed with a light soy sauce marinade to bring out the delicate flavors of the fish meat.

> TOTAL TIME PREP: 15-30 minutes.

Ingredients:

- 2 snow fish fillets
- 2 tablespoons soy sauce
- 1 tablespoon rice wine
- 1 tablespoon vegetable oil
- 1 tablespoon grated ginger
- 2 cloves garlic, minced
- Sliced scallions and cilantro for garnish

Instructions:

1. Place the snow fish fillets in a microwave-safe dish.
2. In a small bowl, whisk together the soy sauce, rice wine, vegetable oil, grated ginger, and minced garlic.
3. Pour the soy sauce mixture over the fish fillets, making sure they are evenly coated.
4. Cover the dish with a microwave-safe plate or lid and microwave on high for 3-4 minutes, until the fish is cooked and no longer translucent.
5. Let the fish cool for a few minutes before garnishing it with sliced scallions and cilantro.
6. Serve with cooked rice.

Stir-Fried Crab With Curry Powder (Poo Pad Pong Garee)

Are you looking for a delicious, flavorful seafood dish to enjoy? Stir-fried crab with curry powder is a great way to experience a delicious meal that's easy to prepare in the comfort of your home. This dish blends the flavors of sweet crab meat, aromatic curry powder and other exciting ingredients into an explosion of flavor that will tantalize your taste buds.

TOTAL TIME PREP: 20 minutes.

Ingredients:

- 2-3 crab meats
- 1 tablespoon curry powder
- 1 tablespoon vegetable oil
- 1/2 onion, sliced
- 2 cloves garlic, minced
- 1/4 cup chicken broth
- 1 tablespoon fish sauce
- 1 tablespoon sugar
- Sliced scallions for garnish

Instructions:

1. In a microwave-safe dish, mix the curry powder and vegetable oil until well combined.
2. Add the sliced onion and minced garlic to the dish and stir to coat with the curry mixture.
3. Microwave the onion and garlic mixture on high for 2-3 minutes or until the onions are tender.
4. Add the crab meat to the dish and the chicken broth, fish sauce, and sugar. Stir to combine everything.
5. Cover the dish with a microwave-safe plate or lid and microwave on high for 3-4 minutes, or until the crab meat is heated through.
6. Let the crab cool for a few minutes before garnishing it with sliced scallions.
7. Serve with cooked rice.

Scrambled Eggs And Green Curry Chicken

Have you ever wanted to try something different for dinner but didn't know what to make? Well, why not try combining two classic dishes into one delicious meal? Scrambled eggs and green curry chicken are great ways to make an entrée with interesting flavors. This combination of savory and spicy will tantalize your taste buds and have your family wanting more. In addition, the dish doesn't take long to prepare and requires only a few ingredients.

TOTAL TIME PREP: 25-30 minutes.

For Scrambled Eggs:

Ingredients:

- 2 large eggs
- 2 tablespoons milk
- 1 tablespoon unsalted butter
- Salt and pepper to taste
- Chopped chives or parsley for garnish (optional)

Instructions:

1. In a microwave-safe bowl, whisk the eggs and milk until well combined.
2. Add the butter to the bowl and microwave on high for 20 seconds, or until the butter is melted.
3. Stir the egg mixture to incorporate the melted butter.
4. Microwave the egg mixture on high for 30 seconds.
5. Remove the bowl from the microwave and stir the eggs.
6. Return the bowl to the microwave and microwave on high for another 30 seconds.
7. Remove the bowl from the microwave and stir the eggs again. If the eggs are still runny, microwave for an additional 15-30 seconds until fully cooked.
8. Season the scrambled eggs with salt and pepper to taste.
9. Garnish with chopped chives or parsley, if desired.

For Green Curry Chicken:

Ingredients:

- 1 lb boneless, skinless chicken breast or thighs, cut into bite-sized pieces
- 2 tablespoons green curry paste
- 1 can (13.5 oz) coconut milk
- 1 tablespoon vegetable oil
- 1 red bell pepper, sliced
- 1 green bell pepper, sliced
- 1 onion, sliced
- 1 tablespoon fish sauce
- 1 tablespoon sugar
- 1/4 cup chopped fresh basil leaves
- Cooked rice, for serving

Instructions:

1. In a large microwave-safe dish, stir the green curry paste and vegetable oil until well combined.
2. Add the chicken pieces to the dish and stir to coat with the curry paste mixture.
3. Add the sliced red and green bell peppers and sliced onion to the dish.
4. Pour the can of coconut milk over the chicken and vegetables.
5. Stir in the fish sauce and sugar.
6. Cover the dish with a microwave-safe lid or plate and microwave on high for 12-15 minutes, until the chicken is cooked and the vegetables are tender.
7. Remove the dish from the microwave and stir in the chopped basil leaves.
8. Serve the scrambled eggs and green curry chicken with cooked rice.

Sweet Eggs Stuffed With Cheese

Eggs are a staple in many diets worldwide, and they can be cooked in various ways. However, for those looking for something extra special, there is no better choice than sweet eggs stuffed with cheese. This easy-to-prepare dish combines the savory flavors of cheese and eggs in one delicious package. Plus, it's a great way to utilize stale bread or leftovers from other meals.

TOTAL TIME PREP: 5 minutes.

Ingredients:

- 2 large eggs
- 1 tablespoon sugar
- Pinch of salt
- 1 oz cream cheese, softened
- 1 tablespoon honey

Instructions:

1. In a microwave-safe bowl, whisk together the eggs, sugar, and salt until well combined.
2. Microwave the egg mixture on high for 1 minute.
3. Remove the bowl from the microwave and stir the eggs.
4. Microwave the egg mixture for another 30 seconds.
5. In a separate bowl, mix the cream cheese and honey.
6. Divide the cream cheese mixture between the two halves of the cooked eggs, spreading it on one side of each.
7. Fold the egg halves over to create a stuffed egg.
8. Microwave the stuffed eggs on high for 30 seconds, or until the cream cheese is melted.
9. Remove the stuffed eggs from the microwave and let them cool for a few minutes before serving.

Baked Macaroni And Cheese

Baked macaroni and cheese is an all-time classic comfort food that's loved by kids and adults alike. It's easy to make and can be customized with different flavors and ingredients, making it a perfect meal for any occasion. With its rich, creamy texture and delicious taste, it's no wonder this dish is so popular! This article will provide an easy-to-follow guide on how to make the perfect baked macaroni and cheese.

TOTAL TIME PREP: 20-25 minutes.

Ingredients:

- 8 oz elbow macaroni
- 2 tablespoons unsalted butter
- 2 tablespoons all-purpose flour
- 1 1/2 cups milk
- 1/2 teaspoon salt
- 1/4 teaspoon black pepper
- 1/4 teaspoon garlic powder
- 1/4 teaspoon onion powder
- 1/4 teaspoon dry mustard
- 1 1/2 cups shredded cheddar cheese
- 1/2 cup breadcrumbs

Instructions:

1. Cook the elbow macaroni according to package instructions until al dente.
2. In a large microwave-safe bowl, melt the butter on high for 30 seconds.
3. Add the flour to the melted butter and stir to combine.
4. Microwave the butter-flour mixture on high for 30 seconds.
5. Gradually whisk in the milk, making sure there are no lumps.
6. Add the salt, black pepper, garlic powder, onion powder, and dry mustard to the bowl and stir to combine.

7. Microwave the mixture on high for 2-3 minutes, or until the mixture has thickened and is bubbly.
8. Stir in the shredded cheddar cheese until melted.
9. Add the cooked elbow macaroni to the cheese sauce and stir to combine.
10. Sprinkle breadcrumbs over the top of the macaroni and cheese.
11. Microwave on high for 2-3 minutes, or until the breadcrumbs are golden brown.
12. Let the macaroni and cheese cool for a few minutes before serving.

Tom Yum Steamed Egg

Tom Yum Steamed Egg is a delicious and unique take on a traditional egg dish. This Thai-inspired recipe will tantalize your taste buds and add an interesting twist to your breakfast, lunch, or dinner. It's incredibly simple to make, requiring only a few ingredients that can be easily found in any grocery store. The savory and spicy flavors make this dish an amazing addition to any meal.

TOTAL TIME PREP: 10 minutes.

Ingredients:

- 2 large eggs
- 1 tablespoon Tom Yum paste
- 1 tablespoon milk
- 1/4 teaspoon salt
- 1/4 teaspoon black pepper
- Chopped green onions for garnish

Instructions:

1. In a microwave-safe bowl, whisk together the eggs, Tom Yum paste, milk, salt, and black pepper until well combined.
2. Cover the bowl with a microwave-safe plate or lid and microwave on high for 1 minute and 30 seconds.
3. Check the egg to see if it has set. If it hasn't, microwave in 30-second increments until set.
4. Once the egg is set, let it cool for a few minutes before garnishing it with chopped green onions.

Garlic Pork

Garlic pork is a succulent and flavorful dish that is enjoyed by many all over the world. This classic yet ever-evolving recipe has been around for centuries, with origins tracing back to China, where it was known as 'Lao Shu Rou.' It is a popular dish in many Asian countries and is renowned for its unique balance of sweet and salty flavors.

> TOTAL TIME PREP: 15-20 minutes.

Ingredients:

- 1 lb boneless pork loin, sliced into bite-sized pieces
- 4 cloves garlic, minced
- 1 tablespoon vegetable oil
- 1 tablespoon soy sauce
- 1 tablespoon oyster sauce
- 1/2 teaspoon sugar
- 1/4 teaspoon black pepper
- Sliced scallions for garnish

Instructions:

1. In a microwave-safe bowl, mix together the minced garlic, vegetable oil, soy sauce, oyster sauce, sugar, and black pepper until well combined.
2. Add the sliced pork to the dish and toss to coat with the garlic mixture.
3. Cover the bowl and microwave on high for 8-10 minutes, or until the pork is cooked through.
4. Remove the bowl from the microwave and let the pork cool for a few minutes before garnishing it with sliced scallions.
5. Serve with cooked rice.

Baked Shrimp With Vermicelli

Shrimp is the perfect addition to various meals, and this baked shrimp with vermicelli recipe is no exception. This delicious dish is easy to prepare and can be enjoyed at any time of the year. The combination of succulent shrimp, savory vegetables, and flavorful spices makes this a meal everyone will love. Not only is it packed full of flavor, but it's also healthy, too - with nutrient-rich ingredients like whole grains and lean protein.

TOTAL TIME PREP: 20-25 minutes.

Ingredients:

- 8 oz vermicelli noodles
- 1/2 lb large shrimp, peeled and deveined
- 1/4 cup chicken broth
- 1 tablespoon vegetable oil
- 2 cloves garlic, minced
- 1 tablespoon fish sauce
- 1 tablespoon sugar
- 1/2 red bell pepper, sliced
- 1/2 green bell pepper, sliced
- Sliced scallions and cilantro for garnish

Instructions:

1. Cook the vermicelli noodles according to package instructions until al dente.
2. In a large microwave-safe dish, mix the chicken broth, vegetable oil, minced garlic, fish sauce, and sugar.
3. Add the cooked vermicelli noodles to the dish and toss to coat with the sauce mixture.
4. Add the sliced red and green bell peppers to the dish.
5. Cover the dish with a microwave-safe lid or plate and microwave on high for 3-4 minutes, or until the vegetables are tender.
6. Add the shrimp to the dish and microwave on high for another 2-3 minutes, or until the shrimp are pink and cooked through.

7. Let the dish cool for a few minutes before garnishing with sliced scallions and cilantro.

Baked Noodles With Cheese

Baked Noodles With Cheese is a delicious and easy dish to make. It's the perfect combination of noodles, cheese, and other ingredients to water your mouth. Not only does this dish taste great, but it also requires minimal preparation and cook time. You can create a delicious meal in no time with just a few simple steps.

TOTAL TIME PREP: 20-25 minutes.

Ingredients:

- 8 oz elbow macaroni or other pasta
- 1/4 cup unsalted butter
- 1/4 cup all-purpose flour
- 2 cups milk
- 1/2 teaspoon salt
- 1/4 teaspoon black pepper
- 1/4 teaspoon garlic powder
- 1/4 teaspoon onion powder
- 1/4 teaspoon dry mustard
- 2 cups shredded cheddar cheese
- 1/4 cup breadcrumbs

Instructions:

1. Cook the elbow macaroni or pasta according to package instructions until al dente.
2. In a large microwave-safe dish, melt the butter on high for 30 seconds.
3. Add the flour to the melted butter and stir to combine.
4. Microwave the butter-flour mixture on high for 30 seconds.
5. Gradually whisk in the milk, making sure there are no lumps.
6. Add the salt, black pepper, garlic powder, onion powder, and dry mustard to the bowl and stir to combine.
7. Microwave the mixture on high for 2-3 minutes or until the mixture has thickened and is bubbly.

8. Stir in the shredded cheddar cheese until melted.
9. Add the cooked elbow macaroni or other pasta to the cheese sauce and stir to combine.
10. Sprinkle breadcrumbs over the top of the macaroni and cheese.
11. Cover the dish with a microwave-safe lid or plate and microwave on high for 3-4 minutes until the breadcrumbs are golden brown and the cheese is bubbly.
12. Let the macaroni and cheese cool for a few minutes before serving.

Seaweed Soup with Tofu

Seaweed soup with tofu is a delicious and easy-to-make dish full of flavor and nutrition. To make this traditional Asian soup, you only need simple ingredients like seaweed, tofu, mushrooms, and vegetables. It's great for vegetarians and can easily be adapted for those who want to add more protein or other ingredients.

TOTAL TIME PREP: 15-20 minutes.

Ingredients:

- 4 cups water
- 1 oz dried seaweed, soaked in water for 10 minutes
- 1/2 onion, sliced
- 2 cloves garlic, minced
- 1 tablespoon vegetable oil
- 1/2 cup sliced mushrooms
- 1/2 cup diced firm tofu
- 1 tablespoon soy sauce
- Salt and pepper to taste
- Sliced scallions for garnish

Instructions:

1. In a microwave-safe dish, microwave the water on high for 3-4 minutes, or until hot.
2. Drain the soaked seaweed and add it to the dish with the hot water.
3. Add the sliced onion and minced garlic to the dish.
4. Microwave the dish on high for 3-4 minutes, or until the onion and garlic are tender.
5. Add the sliced mushrooms and diced tofu to the dish.
6. Microwave the dish on high for another 2-3 minutes, or until the mushrooms are tender and the tofu is heated through.
7. Stir in the soy sauce and season with salt and pepper to taste.
8. Garnish with sliced scallions before serving.
9. Serve with cooked rice.

Lasagna With Meat And Cheese

Lasagna is a classic Italian dish that has been around for centuries. It is typically made with layers of noodles, cheese, and meat to create a savory and satisfying meal. Whether you are cooking for a dinner party or looking for a hearty weeknight dinner, lasagna with meat and cheese will surely please everyone.

TOTAL TIME PREP: 30 minutes.

Ingredients:

- 8 oz lasagna noodles
- 1 lb ground beef
- 1/2 onion, chopped
- 2 cloves garlic, minced
- 1 can (14.5 oz) crushed tomatoes
- 1 can (8 oz) tomato sauce
- 1 tablespoon dried basil
- 1 tablespoon dried oregano
- 1 teaspoon salt
- 1/2 teaspoon black pepper
- 1/2 cup grated Parmesan cheese
- 2 cups shredded mozzarella cheese

Instructions:

1. Cook the lasagna noodles according to package instructions until al dente.
2. In a microwave-safe dish, microwave the ground beef, chopped onion, and minced garlic on high for 6-8 minutes, or until the beef is browned and cooked through.
3. Drain any excess fat from the beef.
4. Add the crushed tomatoes, tomato sauce, dried basil, dried oregano, salt, and black pepper to the dish with the cooked beef and stir to combine.

5. Layer the cooked lasagna noodles on top of the beef and tomato sauce mixture.
6. Sprinkle the grated Parmesan cheese on top of the noodles.
7. Cover the dish with a microwave-safe lid or plate and microwave on high for 6-8 minutes, or until the cheese is melted and bubbly.
8. Let the lasagna cool for a few minutes before serving.

Chicken And Broccoli Casserole

Chicken and Broccoli Casserole is a delicious and easy-to-make weeknight dish that the whole family will love. As a one-pot meal, it is also an excellent solution for busy parents looking for a nutritious, hassle-free dinner. This recipe is deceptively simple to make yet has vibrant flavors that are sure to please even the pickiest eaters in your house.

TOTAL TIME PREP: 30 minutes.

Ingredients:

- 2 tablespoons unsalted butter
- 1/4 cup all-purpose flour
- 1 1/2 cups milk
- 1/2 teaspoon salt
- 1/4 teaspoon black pepper
- 1/4 teaspoon garlic powder
- 1/4 teaspoon onion powder
- 1 lb boneless, skinless chicken breast, cut into bite-sized pieces
- 2 cups chopped broccoli florets
- 1/2 cup shredded cheddar cheese

Instructions:

1. In a separate microwave-safe dish, melt the butter on high for 30 seconds.
2. Add the flour to the melted butter and stir to combine.
3. Microwave the butter-flour mixture on high for 30 seconds.
4. Gradually whisk in the milk, making sure there are no lumps.
5. Add the salt, black pepper, garlic powder, and onion powder to the dish and stir to combine.
6. Add the chicken pieces and chopped broccoli florets with the milk mixture to the dish.
7. Cover the dish with a microwave-safe lid or plate and microwave on high for 10-12 minutes, until the chicken is cooked and the broccoli is tender.

8. Stir in the cooked rice and shredded cheddar cheese.
9. Cover the dish with a microwave-safe lid or plate and microwave on high for 2-3 minutes, or until the cheese is melted and bubbly.
10. Let the casserole cool for a few minutes before serving.
11. Serve with cooked rice.

BBQ Pulled Pork With Slaw And Buns

Are you looking for the perfect way to feed a crowd? Look no further than this delicious BBQ pulled pork recipe. It is easy to prepare and cook, but it also has a smoky flavor that will leave your guests wanting more. This recipe also includes a crunchy slaw and buns to make the perfect sandwich. With its smoky, sweet, and tangy flavors, this BBQ pulled pork dish will surely be a hit at any gathering.

TOTAL TIME PREP: 20-25 minutes.

Ingredients:

- 1 lb pork shoulder or pork butt
- 1/2 cup BBQ sauce
- 1/4 cup water
- 1/4 cup apple cider vinegar
- 1/4 cup brown sugar
- 1/4 teaspoon garlic powder
- 1/4 teaspoon onion powder
- Salt and pepper to taste
- 4 hamburger buns
- 2 cups coleslaw mix

Instructions:

1. In a microwave-safe dish, combine the pork shoulder or pork butt, BBQ sauce, water, apple cider vinegar, brown sugar, garlic powder, onion powder, salt, and pepper.
2. Cover the dish with a microwave-safe lid or plate and microwave on high for 10-12 minutes, or until the pork is tender.
3. Remove the pork from the dish and shred it with two forks.
4. Add the shredded pork to the dish with the sauce and stir to coat.
5. Cover the dish with a microwave-safe lid or plate and microwave on high for another 2-3 minutes, or until the pork is heated and the sauce is bubbly.

6. In a separate microwave-safe dish, microwave the coleslaw mix on high for 2-3 minutes, or until the vegetables are tender.
7. Toast the hamburger buns in a toaster or toaster oven.
8. Serve the pulled pork on the toasted buns and top with the microwaved coleslaw.

Enchiladas With Beef And Cheese

Enchiladas are a classic Mexican dish that can be filled with various delicious ingredients. This particular recipe for enchiladas includes beef, cheese, and sauce, which combine to create an irresistible flavor combination. Whether you're looking for a hearty dinner meal or a tasty snack, this dish will satisfy anyone's appetite. Not only is this recipe incredibly flavorful, but it's also relatively easy to make!

TOTAL TIME PREP: 20-25 minutes.

Ingredients:

- 1 lb ground beef
- 1/2 onion, chopped
- 2 cloves garlic, minced
- 1 can (15 oz) red enchilada sauce
- 8 corn tortillas
- 2 cups shredded cheddar cheese
- Salt and pepper to taste
- Sliced green onions and chopped fresh cilantro for garnish

Instructions:

1. In a microwave-safe dish, microwave the ground beef, chopped onion, and minced garlic on high for 6-8 minutes, or until the meat is browned and cooked through.
2. Drain any excess fat from the beef.
3. Add 1/2 cup of the enchilada sauce to the dish with the cooked beef and stir to combine.
4. Season the beef mixture with salt and pepper to taste.
5. In a separate microwave-safe dish, microwave the corn tortillas on high for 1-2 minutes, or until they are warm and pliable.
6. Spoon a portion of the beef mixture into the center of each tortilla and top with a small amount of shredded cheddar cheese.
7. Roll up the tortillas and place them seam-side down in a microwave-safe baking dish.

8. Pour the remaining enchilada sauce over the rolled-up tortillas and top with the remaining shredded cheddar cheese.
9. Cover the dish with a microwave-safe lid or plate and microwave on high for 6-8 minutes, or until the cheese is melted and bubbly.
10. Garnish with sliced green onions and chopped fresh cilantro before serving.

Bacon-Wrapped Scallops

Bacon-Wrapped Scallops with Lemon and Herbs is a delicious dish anyone can enjoy. It's an easy seafood recipe that combines the flavors of bacon, scallops and various herbs to create an unforgettable one-of-a-kind taste. With just a few ingredients and some simple instructions, you can quickly whip up this crowd-pleasing appetizer or main course in no time.

TOTAL TIME PREP: 20-25 minutes.

Ingredients:

- 1 lb sea scallops
- 8 slices bacon
- 1 lemon, sliced
- 2 tablespoons unsalted butter
- 2 cloves garlic, minced
- 1 tablespoon chopped fresh herbs, such as thyme, rosemary, and parsley
- Salt and pepper to taste

Instructions:

1. Preheat the oven to 375°F (190°C).
2. Wrap each scallop with a slice of bacon and secure it with a toothpick.
3. Place the bacon-wrapped scallops in a microwave-safe dish.
4. Squeeze the juice of half a lemon over the scallops.
5. In a separate microwave-safe dish, melt the butter on high for 30 seconds.
6. Add the minced garlic and chopped fresh herbs to the melted butter and stir to combine.
7. Pour the butter mixture over the bacon-wrapped scallops.
8. Season the scallops with salt and pepper to taste.
9. Top the scallops with the sliced lemon.
10. Cover the dish with a microwave-safe lid or plate and microwave on high for 3-4 minutes, or until the scallops are cooked through.

11. Remove the dish from the microwave and transfer the scallops to a baking sheet.
12. Bake the scallops in the preheated oven for 8-10 minutes, or until the bacon is crispy and the scallops are lightly browned.
13. Let the scallops cool for a few minutes before serving.

Veggie Burger Avocado

Veggie burgers are the perfect meal for anyone looking to make a healthier lifestyle change. Whether you're vegetarian, vegan, or just looking to add more plant-based options to your diet, a veggie burger with avocado and sprouts is a delicious way.

TOTAL TIME PREP: 5-10 minutes.

Ingredients:

- 1 veggie burger patty
- 1 whole wheat hamburger bun
- 1/2 avocado, sliced
- 1/4 cup sprouts
- Salt and pepper to taste

Instructions:

1. Cook the veggie burger patty according to package instructions in the microwave.
2. While the veggie burger cooks, slice the avocado and prepare the sprouts.
3. Toast the hamburger bun in a toaster or toaster oven.
4. Place the veggie burger on the toasted hamburger bun when it is cooked.
5. Top the veggie burger with the sliced avocado and sprouts.
6. Season with salt and pepper to taste.

Stir-Fried Shrimp with Chili and Salt

Stir-frying is a great way to quickly get a delicious, healthy meal on the table. But why not take it one step further and add some extra flavor? Stir-Fried Shrimp with Chili and Salt is a simple but flavorful dish that will impress your family and friends. This easy-to-make recipe uses just a few ingredients but packs an incredible punch of flavor. Not only is it tasty, but shrimp is also low in calories and high in protein.

TOTAL TIME PREP: 10-15 minutes.

Ingredients:

- 1 lb shrimp, peeled and deveined
- 2 tablespoons vegetable oil
- 1 tablespoon chopped garlic
- 1 tablespoon chopped fresh chili pepper
- 1/2 teaspoon salt
- 1/4 teaspoon black pepper
- 2 tablespoons chopped fresh cilantro

Instructions:

1. In a microwave-safe dish, combine the shrimp, vegetable oil, chopped garlic, chopped fresh chili pepper, salt, and black pepper.
2. Stir to combine.
3. Cover the dish with a microwave-safe lid or plate and microwave on high for 3-4 minutes, or until the shrimp are cooked through.
4. Remove the dish from the microwave and stir in the chopped fresh cilantro.
5. Serve the stir-fried shrimp immediately.

Bacon-Wrapped Asparagus Spears

Bacon-wrapped asparagus spears with garlic and parmesan are a delicious and easy side dish that adds extra flavor to any meal. Perfect for busy weeknights, this dish comes together in no time. The smokey bacon, savory parmesan, and lightly charred asparagus will surely be a crowd-pleaser for all ages.

TOTAL TIME PREP: 20-25 minutes.

Ingredients:

- 1 lb asparagus spears, tough ends trimmed
- 8 slices bacon
- 2 cloves garlic, minced
- 1/4 cup grated Parmesan cheese
- Salt and pepper to taste

Instructions:

1. Preheat the oven to 375°F (190°C).
2. Wrap each asparagus spear with a slice of bacon and secure it with a toothpick.
3. Place the bacon-wrapped asparagus spears in a microwave-safe dish.
4. Microwave the asparagus spears on high for 3-4 minutes, or until tender.
5. Remove the dish from the microwave and discard the toothpicks.
6. Sprinkle the minced garlic and grated Parmesan cheese over the asparagus spears.
7. Season the asparagus with salt and pepper to taste.
8. Transfer the asparagus spears to a baking sheet and bake them in the oven for 8-10 minutes, or until the bacon is crispy and the cheese is melted.
9. Let the asparagus cool for a few minutes before serving.

Tuna Spinach Quiche

Tuna Spinach Quiche is a hearty and delicious meal that can be enjoyed for breakfast, lunch, or dinner! This classic quiche combines the rich flavor of tuna with the freshness of spinach for a unique and satisfying dish. It tastes great and is easy to make; you only need a few simple ingredients and about an hour of your time.

TOTAL TIME PREP: 30 minutes.

▪ **Ingredients:**

- 1 pie crust, homemade or store-bought
- 1 can (6 oz) tuna, drained and flaked
- 1 cup fresh spinach leaves, chopped
- 1/2 onion, chopped
- 1/2 red bell pepper, chopped
- 4 eggs
- 1 cup milk
- 1/2 cup shredded cheddar cheese
- Salt and pepper to taste

Instructions:

1. Place the pie crust in a microwave-safe dish and prick the bottom of the crust with a fork.
2. Microwave the pie crust on high for 1-2 minutes, or until it is lightly browned.
3. In a separate microwave-safe dish, microwave the chopped onion and red bell pepper on high for 2-3 minutes, or until they are tender.
4. Add the flaked tuna and chopped spinach to the dish with the onion and red bell pepper.
5. In a separate bowl, whisk together the eggs and milk.
6. Stir the egg mixture into the dish with the tuna, spinach, onion, and red bell pepper.
7. Season the mixture with salt and pepper to taste.
8. Pour the tuna and egg mixture into the pie crust.

9. Sprinkle the shredded cheddar cheese over the top of the mixture.
10. Cover the dish with a microwave-safe lid or plate and microwave on high for 8-10 minutes, or until the quiche is set and the cheese is melted and bubbly.
11. Let the quiche cool for a few minutes before serving.

Whole Wheat Seafood Pizza

Pizza is a classic dish many love, but it's not always the healthiest option. That's why Whole Wheat Seafood Pizza is the perfect solution for those seeking a healthier alternative to traditional pizza. This unique pizza combines flavorful seafood ingredients with nutritious whole wheat dough for an irresistible combination of taste and nutrition. The result is a delicious meal satisfying any craving without skimping on flavor.

TOTAL TIME PREP: 15-20 minutes.

Ingredients:

- 1 whole wheat pizza crust, homemade or store-bought
- 1/2 cup tomato sauce
- 1/2 cup shredded mozzarella cheese
- 1/2 lb seafood, such as shrimp, scallops, and calamari
- 1/4 red onion, thinly sliced
- 1/4 cup sliced black olives
- 2 tablespoons chopped fresh parsley
- Salt and pepper to taste

Instructions:

1. Place the whole wheat pizza crust on a microwave-safe plate.
2. Spread the tomato sauce over the pizza crust.
3. Sprinkle the shredded mozzarella cheese over the tomato sauce.
4. Add the seafood, sliced red onion, and sliced black olives to the pizza.
5. Season with salt and pepper to taste.
6. Cover the plate with a microwave-safe lid or plate and microwave on high for 5-7 minutes, or until the cheese is melted and bubbly and the crust is crispy.
7. Remove the plate from the microwave and sprinkle the chopped fresh parsley over the top of the pizza.
8. Let the pizza cool for a few minutes before serving.

Mini Ham Cheese Pizza

Mini Ham Cheese Pizza is a delicious and easy-to-make meal for the whole family. Whether you're looking for a quick lunch or dinner, this classic Italian recipe is a great option. It's packed with protein, vitamins and minerals, yet doesn't skimp on flavor. Its simple ingredients make it ideal for busy days or rushed meals, but don't let its size fool you - this mini pizza packs a lot of taste into one bite!

TOTAL TIME PREP: 10-15 minutes.

Ingredients:

- 4 mini pizza crusts, homemade or store-bought
- 1/2 cup tomato sauce
- 1 cup shredded mozzarella cheese
- 1/2 cup diced ham
- 2 tablespoons chopped fresh parsley
- Salt and pepper to taste

Instructions:

1. Place the mini pizza crusts on a microwave-safe plate.
2. Spread the tomato sauce over each pizza crust.
3. Sprinkle the shredded mozzarella cheese over the tomato sauce.
4. Add the diced ham to top of the cheese.
5. Season with salt and pepper to taste.
6. Cover the plate with a microwave-safe lid or plate and microwave on high for 2-3 minutes, or until the cheese is melted and bubbly and the crust is crispy.
7. Remove the plate from the microwave and sprinkle the chopped fresh parsley over the top of the pizzas.
8. Let the mini pizzas cool for a few minutes before serving.

Pizza Zucchini

Pizza Zucchini is a delicious, nutritious dish that will surely please everyone in the family. It combines the best of Italian and healthy ingredients that can be whipped up quickly. This tasty alternative to traditional pizza is a great way to incorporate more vegetables into your diet while enjoying your favorite flavors.

TOTAL TIME PREP: 10-15 minutes.

Ingredients:

- 2 medium zucchinis, sliced lengthwise
- 1/2 cup tomato sauce
- 1 cup shredded mozzarella cheese
- 1/4 cup sliced black olives
- 1/4 cup sliced pepperoni
- Salt and pepper to taste

Instructions:

1. Place the sliced zucchinis on a microwave-safe plate.
2. Spread the tomato sauce over each zucchini slice.
3. Sprinkle the shredded mozzarella cheese over the tomato sauce.
4. Add the sliced black olives and pepperoni on top of the cheese.
5. Season with salt and pepper to taste.
6. Cover the plate with a microwave-safe lid or plate and microwave on high for 5-7 minutes, or until the cheese is melted and bubbly and the zucchini is tender.
7. Remove the plate from the microwave and let it cool for a few minutes before serving.

Tuna Pumpkin Scrambled Eggs

For a unique breakfast experience, try Tuna Pumpkin Scrambled Eggs! This delicious combination creates a tasty and nutritious meal that will make your morning special. In addition, it is surprisingly easy to make, requiring only a few simple ingredients and minimal preparation time. The result is a dish that has the perfect balance of salty and sweet, with the added bonus of being high in protein and fiber.

TOTAL TIME PREP: 10-15 minutes.

Ingredients:

- 1 cup pumpkin puree
- 4 eggs
- 1 can (6 oz) tuna, drained and flaked
- 1/4 cup milk
- 2 tablespoons unsalted butter
- Salt and pepper to taste

Instructions:

1. In a microwave-safe dish, combine the pumpkin puree, eggs, flaked tuna, milk, unsalted butter, salt, and pepper.
2. Whisk the mixture together until well combined.
3. Cover the dish with a microwave-safe lid or plate and microwave on high for 3-4 minutes, until the eggs are cooked and the mixture is set.
4. Remove the dish from the microwave and let it cool for a few minutes before serving.

Steamed Egg With Vegetables And Shrimp

Eggs are a staple food in many cultures and cuisines around the world. They are also easy to prepare and can be used as the main ingredient for various dishes. This article will explore one such dish - steamed egg with vegetables and shrimp. This delicious recipe combines eggs, vegetables and shrimp in a savory, nutritious, and flavorful combination.

TOTAL TIME PREP: 10-15 minutes.

Ingredients:

- 3 eggs
- 1/2 cup cooked shrimp, chopped
- 1/2 cup mixed vegetables, such as carrots, peas, and corn
- 1 tablespoon chopped scallions
- 1 tablespoon soy sauce
- 1/2 teaspoon sesame oil
- 1/2 teaspoon salt
- 1/4 teaspoon black pepper

Instructions:

1. In a microwave-safe dish, combine the eggs, chopped shrimp, mixed vegetables, chopped scallions, soy sauce, sesame oil, salt, and black pepper.
2. Whisk the mixture together until well combined.
3. Cover the dish with a microwave-safe lid or plate and microwave on high for 3-4 minutes, until the egg is cooked and the mixture is set.
4. Remove the dish from the microwave and let it cool for a few minutes before serving.

Mediterranean Tuna Salad

Tuna salad is a classic staple of Mediterranean cuisine enjoyed by many across the region. This easy-to-make dish has existed for centuries, and its popularity continues today. Mediterranean Tuna Salad is a delicious combination of tuna, vegetables, and flavorful herbs, creating a nutritious and tasty meal. Not only is it full of flavor, but it also provides essential vitamins and minerals to help keep you healthy.

TOTAL TIME PREP: 10-15 minutes.

Ingredients:

- 1 can (6 oz) tuna, drained and flaked
- 1/2 cup cooked chickpeas
- 1/2 cup diced cucumber
- 1/2 cup cherry tomatoes, halved
- 1/4 cup sliced black olives
- 2 tablespoons chopped fresh parsley
- 2 tablespoons lemon juice
- 2 tablespoons olive oil
- Salt and pepper to taste

Instructions:

1. In a microwave-safe dish, combine the flaked tuna, cooked chickpeas, diced cucumber, halved cherry tomatoes, sliced black olives, chopped fresh parsley, lemon juice, olive oil, salt, and pepper.
2. Stir the mixture together until well combined.
3. Cover the dish with a microwave-safe lid or plate and microwave on high for 2-3 minutes, or until the vegetables are tender and the tuna is warmed through.
4. Remove the dish from the microwave and let it cool for a few minutes before serving.

Stir-Fried Mixed Vegetables

Eating healthy is an important part of a balanced lifestyle, and stir-fried mixed vegetables are the perfect way to get nutrients. This delicious dish is easy to make, requires minimal ingredients and can be easily tailored to your tastes. Not only is it full of flavor, but it also boasts a range of vitamins and minerals that provide numerous health benefits.

TOTAL TIME PREP: 10-15 minutes.

Ingredients:

- 2 cups mixed vegetables, such as broccoli, bell peppers, carrots, and snap peas
- 1 tablespoon vegetable oil
- 1 tablespoon soy sauce
- 1/2 teaspoon sesame oil
- 1/4 teaspoon garlic powder
- Salt and pepper to taste

Instructions:

1. In a microwave-safe dish, combine the mixed vegetables, vegetable oil, soy sauce, sesame oil, garlic powder, salt, and pepper.
2. Stir the mixture together until the vegetables are evenly coated.
3. Cover the dish with a microwave-safe lid or plate and microwave on high for 4-5 minutes, stirring halfway through, or until the vegetables are tender and cooked through.
4. Remove the dish from the microwave and let it cool for a few minutes before serving.

Curry Beef

Curry beef is a classic dish that has been enjoyed in households around the world for generations. It is a flavorful and hearty meal, making it an ideal dinner for any night of the week. Curry beef combines succulent beef, fragrant spices, and creamy coconut milk to create a dish that is both comforting and delicious. This recipe can be easily adjusted to personal taste preferences, so it's perfect for families who like to customize their meals.

TOTAL TIME PREP: 10-15 minutes.

Ingredients:

- 1 lb beef, sliced into thin strips
- 1 onion, chopped
- 2 tablespoons curry powder
- 1 can (14 oz) coconut milk
- 1 tablespoon vegetable oil
- Salt and pepper to taste

Instructions:

1. In a microwave-safe dish, combine the sliced beef, chopped onion, curry powder, coconut milk, vegetable oil, salt, and pepper.
2. Stir the mixture together until well combined.
3. Cover the dish with a microwave-safe lid or plate and microwave on high for 10-12 minutes, stirring occasionally, or until the beef is cooked and the curry is heated.
4. Remove the dish from the microwave and let it cool for a few minutes before serving.
5. Serve with cooked rice.

Tom Yum Canned Fish

Tom Yum Canned Fish is an exciting, flavorful twist on the classic Thai dish. This delicious canned fish packs a punch of flavor with only a few ingredients. With just the right combination of tart and spicy, Tom Yum Canned Fish offers an authentic experience that can be enjoyed at any time. Not only is this dish delicious, but it's also very convenient to make and requires minimal prep work.

TOTAL TIME PREP: 10-15 minutes.

Ingredients:

- 1 can (6 oz) fish, such as mackerel or tuna
- 1/2 cup water
- 2 tablespoons Tom Yum paste
- 1/4 cup sliced mushrooms
- 1/4 cup sliced fresh tomatoes
- 1 tablespoon fish sauce
- 1 tablespoon lime juice
- 1 tablespoon sliced fresh cilantro

1. **Instructions:**
2. In a microwave-safe dish, combine the canned fish, water, Tom Yum paste, sliced mushrooms, chopped fresh tomatoes, fish sauce, and lime juice.
3. Stir the mixture together until well combined.
4. Cover the dish with a microwave-safe lid or plate and microwave on high for 3-4 minutes, or until the fish is heated through and the vegetables are tender.
5. Remove the dish from the microwave and let it cool for a few minutes before serving.
6. Sprinkle chopped fresh cilantro over the top of the dish before serving.
7. Serve with cooked rice.

Marinated Chicken Breast with Red Sauce

Cooking a delicious meal for friends and family doesn't have to be complicated or time-consuming. This marinated chicken breast with red sauce recipe is the perfect example of an easy-to-make yet flavorful dish. The marinade only requires simple ingredients, and the red sauce uses essential store-bought ingredients.

> TOTAL TIME PREP: 15-20 minutes.

Ingredients:

- 2 boneless, skinless chicken breasts
- 1/2 cup red sauce, such as tomato sauce or marinara sauce
- 2 tablespoons balsamic vinegar
- 2 tablespoons olive oil
- 1 teaspoon dried oregano
- 1 teaspoon dried basil
- 1/2 teaspoon garlic powder
- Salt and pepper to taste

Instructions:

1. In a microwave-safe dish, whisk together the red sauce, balsamic vinegar, olive oil, dried oregano, dried basil, garlic powder, salt, and pepper.
2. Add the chicken breasts to the marinade, ensuring they are evenly coated.
3. Cover the dish with a microwave-safe lid or plate and microwave on high for 8-10 minutes, flipping the chicken breasts halfway through, or until the chicken is cooked through and the sauce is heated through.
4. Remove the dish from the microwave and serve with cooked rice.

** Dessert Recipe **

Banana Cake

Banana cake is a delicious and popular dessert that is enjoyed all around the world. It is a moist, sweet, and flavorful cake made with ripe bananas, giving it a unique taste and texture. This type of cake is a favorite among many people, and it is commonly served as a dessert or a sweet treat for breakfast or afternoon tea. Banana cake is also a great way to use overripe bananas that might otherwise go to waste.

TOTAL TIME PREP: 15-20 minutes.

Ingredients:

- 2 ripe bananas, mashed
- 1/2 cup sugar
- 1/4 cup vegetable oil
- 1 egg
- 1/2 teaspoon vanilla extract
- 1/2 cup all-purpose flour
- 1/2 teaspoon baking powder
- 1/2 teaspoon baking soda
- Pinch of salt

Instructions:

1. In a microwave-safe mixing bowl, combine the mashed bananas, sugar, vegetable oil, egg, and vanilla extract.
2. Mix until well combined.
3. Add the all-purpose flour, baking powder, baking soda, and a pinch of salt.
4. Mix until just combined, being careful not to overmix.
5. Pour the mixture into a microwave-safe cake pan.
6. Cover the pan with a microwave-safe lid or plate and microwave on high for 5-7 minutes, or until the cake is set.
7. Remove the pan from the microwave and let the cake cool for a few minutes before slicing and serving.

Banana Cake (Flourless Recipe)

Banana cake is a delicious and popular dessert that is enjoyed all around the world. It is a moist, sweet, and flavorful cake made with ripe bananas, giving it a unique taste and texture. This type of cake is a favorite among many people, and it is commonly served as a dessert or a sweet treat for breakfast or afternoon tea. Banana cake is also a great way to use overripe bananas that might otherwise go to waste.

TOTAL TIME PREP: 10-15 minutes.

Ingredients:

- 2 ripe bananas, mashed
- 2 eggs
- 1/2 cup almond butter (or any nut butter)
- 1/4 cup honey
- 1/2 teaspoon baking powder
- 1/2 teaspoon cinnamon

Instructions:

1. In a microwave-safe mixing bowl, combine the mashed bananas, eggs, almond butter, honey, baking powder, and cinnamon.
2. Mix until well combined.
3. Pour the mixture into a microwave-safe cake pan.
4. Cover the pan with a microwave-safe lid or plate and microwave on high for 5-6 minutes, or until the cake is set.
5. Remove the pan from the microwave and let the cake cool for a few minutes before slicing and serving.

Baked Banana with Butter and Honey

Baked banana with butter and honey is a simple and delicious dessert perfect for those who love the banana's sweet and natural flavor. This dessert is incredibly easy to make and requires only a few ingredients, making it a great option for a quick and satisfying dessert or snack.

TOTAL TIME PREP: 5-10 minutes.

Ingredients:

- 2 ripe bananas, peeled and sliced lengthwise
- 2 tablespoons unsalted butter, melted
- 2 tablespoons honey
- 1/2 teaspoon cinnamon

Instructions:

1. Place the sliced bananas in a microwave-safe dish.
2. Drizzle the melted butter over the top of the bananas.
3. Drizzle the honey over the top of the bananas.
4. Sprinkle the cinnamon over the top of the bananas.
5. Cover the dish with a microwave-safe lid or plate and microwave on high for 2-3 minutes, or until the bananas are tender and the butter and honey are bubbly.
6. Remove the dish from the microwave and let it cool for a few minutes before serving.

Blueberry Cheese Pie

Blueberry cheese pie is a classic and mouth-watering dessert that combines the sweet tanginess of blueberries with the rich creaminess of the cheese. It is a popular dessert in many parts of the world, especially during the summer months when blueberries are in season. Blueberry cheese pie can be served as a refreshing and indulgent treat for a special occasion or as a sweet end to a family dinner.

TOTAL TIME PREP: 20-25 minutes.

Ingredients:

- 1 pre-made pie crust
- 8 oz cream cheese, softened
- 1/2 cup sugar
- 1 egg
- 1/2 teaspoon vanilla extract
- 1 cup fresh blueberries
- 2 tablespoons all-purpose flour
- 2 tablespoons sugar
- 1/2 teaspoon cinnamon

Instructions:

1. Place the pre-made pie crust in a microwave-safe pie dish.
2. In a separate mixing bowl, combine the softened cream cheese, 1/2 cup sugar, egg, and vanilla extract.
3. Whisk the mixture together until well combined.
4. Pour the cream cheese mixture into the pre-made pie crust.
5. In a separate mixing bowl, combine the fresh blueberries, all-purpose flour, 2 tablespoons of sugar, and cinnamon.
6. Stir the mixture together until the blueberries are evenly coated.
7. Pour the blueberry mixture over the top of the cream cheese mixture into the pie crust.

8. Cover the pie with a microwave-safe lid or plate and microwave on high for 6-8 minutes, or until the pie is set and the blueberries are bubbling.
9. Remove the pie from the microwave and let it cool for a few minutes before serving.

Creme Brulee

Creme Brulee is a classic French dessert that has become popular all over the world for its decadent and creamy texture and the satisfying crunch of its caramelized sugar topping. Creme Brulee is a dessert that can be enjoyed in fancy restaurants or made at home for a special occasion or a romantic dinner.

TOTAL TIME PREP: 30 minutes.

Ingredients:

- 2 cups heavy cream
- 1/2 cup sugar
- 1 teaspoon vanilla extract
- 4 egg yolks
- 4 tablespoons brown sugar

Instructions:

1. In a microwave-safe mixing bowl, combine the heavy cream, sugar, and vanilla extract.
2. Microwave on high for 4-5 minutes until the mixture is hot but not boiling.
3. In a separate mixing bowl, whisk the egg yolks together until smooth.
4. Slowly pour the hot cream mixture into the bowl with the egg yolks, constantly whisking to combine.
5. Strain the mixture through a fine-mesh strainer to remove any lumps or solids.
6. Divide the mixture evenly among 4 microwave-safe ramekins or custard cups.
7. Cover the ramekins or custard cups with microwave-safe plastic wrap.
8. Microwave on medium power for 5-6 minutes until the mixture is set but still slightly jiggly in the center.

9. Remove the ramekins or custard cups from the microwave and let them cool to room temperature.
10. Sprinkle 1 tablespoon of brown sugar over the top of each creme brulee.
11. Use a kitchen torch to caramelize the sugar until it is golden brown and bubbly.
12. Let the creme brulees cool for a few minutes before serving.

Banoffee

Banoffee is a delicious and unique dessert that combines the sweetness of bananas and toffee with the creaminess of whipped cream. Originating in England during the 1970s, it has since become a popular flavor around the world. This article explores the history of banoffee, its ingredients, and recipes for making this decadent treat. It also offers some creative variations to make this beloved dessert even more delicious.

TOTAL TIME PREP: 15-20 minutes.

Ingredients:

- 1 pre-made graham cracker crust
- 1 can (14 oz) sweetened condensed milk
- 2 ripe bananas, sliced
- 1 cup heavy cream
- 2 tablespoons sugar
- 1/2 teaspoon vanilla extract

Instructions:

1. Pour the sweetened condensed milk into a microwave-safe bowl.
2. Microwave on high for 3-4 minutes, stirring every 30 seconds, until the milk is caramelized and thickened.
3. Pour the caramelized milk into the pre-made graham cracker crust.
4. Arrange the sliced bananas over the top of the caramelized milk.
5. In a separate mixing bowl, whisk the heavy cream, sugar, and vanilla extract together until stiff peaks form.
6. Spread the whipped cream over the top of the bananas.
7. Cover the pie with a microwave-safe lid or plate and microwave on high for 3-4 minutes, or until the whipped cream is set and the bananas are tender.
8. Remove the pie from the microwave and let it cool for a few minutes before serving.

Cheese Pie Lime

Cheese Pie Lime is a delicious dessert that will tantalize your taste buds! This unique and flavorful pie is the perfect treat for any special occasion. Its light and creamy texture and zesty lime flavor make it an irresistible dish that everyone will enjoy. In addition, this recipe is quick and easy to make, so you can whip up a batch of this delightful treat in no time.

TOTAL TIME PREP: 20-25 minutes.

Ingredients:

- 1 pre-made pie crust
- 8 oz cream cheese, softened
- 1/2 cup sugar
- 2 eggs
- 1/4 cup fresh lime juice
- 1 tablespoon grated lime zest

Instructions:

1. Place the pre-made pie crust in a microwave-safe pie dish.
2. In a separate mixing bowl, combine the softened cream cheese, 1/2 cup sugar, and eggs.
3. Whisk the mixture together until well-combined.
4. Add the fresh lime juice and grated lime zest to the cream cheese mixture.
5. Whisk the mixture again until well-combined.
6. Pour the mixture into the pre-made pie crust.
7. Cover the pie with a microwave-safe lid or plate and microwave on high for 6-8 minutes, or until the pie is set and the edges are slightly golden.
8. Remove the pie from the microwave and let it cool for a few minutes before serving.

Nama Chocolate Green Tea

Nama Chocolate Green Tea is the perfect combination of sweet and bitter flavors, sure to tantalize your taste buds. This unique Japanese-style tea is made from high-quality Matcha green tea leaves and rich cocoa powder, resulting in a delicious harmony of flavors. Nama Chocolate Green Tea has been gaining popularity due to its unique flavor profile and health benefits. In addition, it can be served either hot or cold, making it an excellent beverage for all seasons.

TOTAL TIME PREP: 15-20 minutes.

Ingredients:

- 1/2 cup heavy cream
- 8 oz high-quality white chocolate, chopped
- 1 tablespoon green tea powder (matcha)
- Cocoa powder for dusting

Instructions:

1. In a microwave-safe mixing bowl, heat the heavy cream in the microwave for 1-2 minutes or until hot but not boiling.
2. Add the chopped white chocolate to the hot cream and stir until the chocolate is melted and the mixture is smooth.
3. Add the green tea powder to the chocolate mixture and stir until it is well combined.
4. Pour the mixture into a shallow, microwave-safe dish or mold.
5. Cover the dish or mold with microwave-safe plastic wrap and microwave on high for 1-2 minutes or until the chocolate is set.
6. Remove the dish or mold from the microwave and let the chocolate cool to room temperature.
7. Once the chocolate has cooled, dust the surface with cocoa powder.
8. Cut the chocolate into bite-sized pieces and serve.

French Toast Honey

French toast is a beloved breakfast staple that can be enjoyed in various ways. From savory to sweet, this warm and comforting meal is a favorite for people of all ages. One especially popular variation on the classic French toast dish is French Toast Honey, which adds a touch of sweetness with a healthy helping of honey. This recipe is simple to make while still being incredibly delicious and satisfying.

TOTAL TIME PREP: 5-10 minutes.

Ingredients:

- 2 slices bread
- 1 egg
- 1/4 cup milk
- 1 tablespoon honey
- 1/2 teaspoon vanilla extract
- Pinch of salt
- Butter
- Maple syrup and extra honey, for serving
- Whipped cream, Ice cream and fresh strawberries (optional)

Instructions:

1. In a microwave-safe mixing bowl, whisk together the egg, milk, honey, vanilla extract, and salt.
2. Dip the bread slices into the egg mixture, making sure they are coated evenly on both sides.
3. Grease a microwave-safe dish with butter.
4. Place the coated bread slices in the greased dish.
5. Cover the dish with microwave-safe plastic wrap and microwave on high for 1-2 minutes, or until the bread is cooked through and the egg mixture is set.
6. Remove the dish from the microwave and let it cool for a few minutes.
7. Drizzle with additional honey and maple syrup before serving.

8. Garnish the toast with a dollop of whipped cream, Ice cream and fresh strawberries, if desired.

Brownies (Crispy Face)

Brownies are a classic treat that has been enjoyed for generations. Whether you prefer chewy or cakey, topped with frosting or plain, there is an option to suit every palate. While homemade brownies are always a favorite, store-bought options can be just as tasty and convenient. As a dessert staple, brownies have been gracing the tables of family gatherings, potlucks, and social events for years.

TOTAL TIME PREP: 15-20 minutes.

Ingredients:

- 1/2 cup unsalted butter
- 1 cup granulated sugar
- 1/2 cup all-purpose flour
- 1/2 cup unsweetened cocoa powder
- 2 eggs
- 1/4 teaspoon baking powder
- 1/4 teaspoon salt
- 1/2 teaspoon vanilla extract
- 1/4 cup chocolate chips

Instructions:

1. In a microwave-safe mixing bowl, melt the butter in the microwave for 30-45 seconds, or until completely melted.
2. Add the granulated sugar to the melted butter and whisk until well combined.
3. Add the flour, cocoa powder, eggs, baking powder, salt, and vanilla extract to the butter mixture.
4. Whisk the mixture until it is smooth and there are no lumps.
5. Stir in the chocolate chips.
6. Pour the mixture into a microwave-safe dish, making sure it is evenly distributed.
7. Microwave on high for 3-5 minutes, or until the brownies are set.

8. Remove the dish from the microwave and let it cool for a few minutes.
9. Dust the top of the brownies with cocoa powder.
10. Cut into bite-sized pieces and serve.

Honey Toast

Honey toast is a popular sweet snack that originated in Japan. It's a simple yet delicious dish, made with pieces of toast topped with honey and other sweet ingredients. This easy-to-make treat has become increasingly popular around the world, as it can be enjoyed any time of day. So whether you're looking for a quick breakfast before work or a yummy dessert after dinner, honey toast is the perfect solution!

TOTAL TIME PREP: 5-10 minutes.

Ingredients:

- 2 slices bread, preferably thick slices
- Butter
- Honey
- whipped cream, Ice cream and fresh fruits (optional)

Instructions:

1. Spread a thin layer of butter on each slice of bread.
2. Place the bread slices on a microwave-safe plate.
3. Microwave on high for 10-20 seconds, or until they are lightly golden.
4. Remove the plate from the microwave and Drizzle honey over the top of the bread slices.
5. Serve the toast with a dollop of whipped cream, Ice cream and fresh fruits, if desired.

Fresh Cream Strawberry Mochi

Welcome to the world of Fresh Cream Strawberry Mochi, a delightful and delicious Japanese dessert! This delectable treat is made from chewy mochi rice cakes that are filled with fresh cream and sweet strawberry jam. Its unique texture and flavor make it an interesting and enjoyable snack or dessert. With its bold colors and fun shapes, this mochi will surely be a hit at any gathering or party.

TOTAL TIME PREP: 20-25 minutes.

Ingredients:

- 1 cup glutinous rice flour
- 1/4 cup granulated sugar
- 1/2 cup water
- 1/2 cup cornstarch
- 1/4 cup powdered sugar
- 1/2 cup heavy cream
- 1/2 cup chopped strawberries

Instructions:

1. In a microwave-safe mixing bowl, combine the glutinous rice flour, granulated sugar, and water.
2. Stir the mixture until it forms a smooth, sticky dough.
3. Cover the dough with microwave-safe plastic wrap and microwave on high for 2-3 minutes, or until the dough is cooked through.
4. In a separate mixing bowl, combine the cornstarch and powdered sugar.
5. Sprinkle cornstarch mixtures on a flat surface and roll the cooked dough into a thin, even layer.
6. Cut the dough into small, bite-sized pieces.
7. In another mixing bowl, whip the heavy cream until stiff peaks form.
8. Add the chopped strawberries to the whipped cream and mix until well combined.

9. Place a small amount of the strawberry cream filling in the center of each dough piece.
10. Fold the dough over the filling and pinch the edges together to seal.
11. Dust the mochi pieces with the remaining cornstarch mixture to prevent sticking.
12. Serve the fresh cream strawberry mochi immediately.

Apple Crumble Cake

Apple Crumble Cake is a classic dessert recipe passed down for generations. This fall favorite combines the sweet flavor of apples with the satisfying crunch of a crumb topping. It's easy to make and a delicious way to use up any extra apples from your tree. Apple Crumble Cake is a tasty treat and has a nostalgic charm that will bring back fond memories of times spent in the kitchen with family.

TOTAL TIME PREP: 20-25 minutes.

Ingredients:

- 2 cups all-purpose flour
- 1 cup granulated sugar
- 1/2 cup unsalted butter, softened
- 2 eggs
- 1 teaspoon baking powder
- 1/2 teaspoon baking soda
- 1/2 teaspoon salt
- 1 teaspoon ground cinnamon
- 1/4 teaspoon ground nutmeg
- 2 cups chopped apples
- 1/2 cup rolled oats
- 1/4 cup brown sugar
- 1/4 cup unsalted butter, melted

Instructions:

1. In a microwave-safe mixing bowl, cream together the all-purpose flour, granulated sugar, and softened butter.
2. Add the eggs to the mixture and beat until well combined.
3. Stir in the baking powder, baking soda, salt, cinnamon, and nutmeg.
4. Fold in the chopped apples.
5. Pour the mixture into a microwave-safe dish, making sure it is evenly distributed.

6. In a separate mixing bowl, combine the rolled oats, brown sugar, and melted butter to make the crumble topping.
7. Sprinkle the crumble topping over the top of the apple cake mixture.
8. Cover the dish with microwave-safe plastic wrap and microwave on high for 8-10 minutes, or until the cake is set and the topping is crispy.
9. Remove the dish from the microwave and let it cool for a few minutes before serving.

Apple Turnovers Cinnamon

Nothing quite compares to the aroma of Apple Turnovers with Cinnamon and Sugar baking in the oven. This classic dessert is as delicious as it is simple to make, making it a perfect option for busy weeknights or special occasions. Combining sweet apples, buttery pastry, and fragrant cinnamon sugar creates an irresistible flavor that your family will ask for seconds.

TOTAL TIME PREP: 20-25 minutes.

Ingredients:

- 2 sheets frozen puff pastry, thawed
- 2 cups chopped apples
- 1/4 cup granulated sugar
- 1 teaspoon ground cinnamon
- 1 egg, beaten
- Turbinado sugar, for sprinkling

Instructions:

1. In a microwave-safe mixing bowl, combine the chopped apples, granulated sugar, and ground cinnamon.
2. Microwave on high for 5-7 minutes, or until the apples are soft and tender.
3. Roll out the thawed puff pastry sheets on a floured surface.
4. Cut each sheet into 4 equal squares.
5. Place a spoonful of the cooked apple mixture on each square of pastry.
6. Brush the edges of the pastry with beaten egg.
7. Fold the pastry over the filling to form a triangle.
8. Press the edges together with a fork to seal.
9. Place the turnovers on a microwave-safe plate.
10. Brush the top of each turnover with more beaten egg and sprinkle with turbinado sugar.
11. Microwave on high for 5-7 minutes, or until the pastry is golden brown and crispy.

12. Remove the plate from the microwave and let it cool for a few minutes before serving.

Caramel Pudding

Caramel pudding is a classic dessert that has delighted the taste buds of many for decades. It features a creamy, golden-brown center that is sweet and rich in flavor. In addition, caramel pudding is surprisingly easy to make, requiring only a few simple ingredients. The result is a delicious treat that can be enjoyed alone or served with cream or ice cream for an extra special indulgence.

TOTAL TIME PREP: 30 minutes.

Ingredients:

- 1 cup granulated sugar
- 1/2 cup water
- 2 cups milk
- 4 eggs
- 1 teaspoon vanilla extract

Instructions:

1. In a microwave-safe mixing bowl, combine the granulated sugar and water.
2. Microwave on high for 6-8 minutes, or until the mixture turns golden brown and caramelized.
3. Carefully pour the caramel into a microwave-safe dish, making sure it is evenly distributed across the bottom.
4. In a separate mixing bowl, whisk together the milk, eggs, and vanilla extract.
5. Pour the milk mixture into the caramel-coated dish.
6. Cover the dish with microwave-safe plastic wrap and microwave on medium power for 10-12 minutes, or until the pudding is set and a toothpick inserted into the center comes out clean.
7. Remove the dish from the microwave and let it cool to room temperature.
8. Once the pudding has cooled, invert the dish onto a plate to release the pudding. Slice the pudding and serve.

<u>NOTE:</u>

Printed in Great Britain
by Amazon